YOU'D *never* BELIEVE IT BUT...

water has a skin

and other facts about water

© Aladdin Books Ltd 1998

Designed and produced by
Aladdin Books Ltd
28 Percy Street
London W1P 0LD

First published in Great Britain in 1998 by
Aladdin Books/Watts Books
96 Leonard Street
London EC2A 4RH

Designed by

David West • Children's Books
Designer
Flick Killerby
Computer illustrations
Stephen Sweet (Simon Girling & Associates)
Picture Research
Brooks Krikler Research
Project Editor
Sally Hewitt
Editor
Sarah Levete

ISBN 0-7496-3252-6

Printed in Belgium

A CIP catalogue record for this book is
available from the British Library.

YOU'D *never* BELIEVE IT BUT...

water has a skin

and other facts about water

Helen Taylor

ALADDIN/WATTS
LONDON • SYDNEY

Contents

What is water? 6
Water on Earth 8
Liquid water 10
Solid water 12
Water in the air 14
The weather 16
The water cycle 18
Floating and sinking 20
Mixing and dissolving 22
Water in your body 24
Washing 26
Living in water 28
Glossary 30
Index 32

Introduction

Water from the tap, ice from the freezer and

mist in the air – these are all different forms of water. All human, animal and plant life on Earth needs water for survival.

Join Jack and Jo as they discover all about water, from how water is used up again and again to how soap and water help to keep you clean.

FUN PROJECTS
Wherever you see this sign, it means there is a fun project which you can do. Each project will help you to understand more about the subject.

WARNING:
Water is fun, but it can be very dangerous. Only play or go near water when a grown-up is present.

What is water?

Water is everywhere. It fills the seas and rivers, it is in the ground and it is in the air.

You can see or feel water in three different ways. It can be a liquid, like the water you drink. It can be a solid, like ice in the fridge. It can also be a gas, like steam.

What has no taste, no smell and no colour?

Water. But it feels wet!

In a liquid form, like water from a tap, water feels wet.

In a solid form, as ice, water feels cold and hard.

Water becomes a gas when it gets very hot. This gas is called steam.

You'd never believe it but...

Water can make electricity. The power or energy from fast-flowing water or steam can be used to make electricity.

Water on Earth

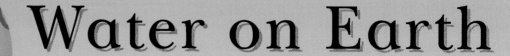

Earth, the planet we live on, is covered by much more water than land!

All living things need water to live and grow.

Can you imagine what our planet might be like with no water?

Most of the water on Earth is salty seawater. Seawater is salty because it contains minerals and salts washed off the land and carried to the sea.

Without water nothing would grow.

The water in rivers, streams and lakes is not salty. We call it freshwater. This is the water we drink and that most plants need to grow.

You'd never believe it but...

There is no liquid water on the moon, only ice. Nothing can grow on the moon. Earth might look like the moon if it had no liquid water.

The water in the sea is very salty. Only sea creatures and sea plants can live in the sea. Have you ever tasted salty water? It's not good to drink!

All the plants would die.

WATERING PLANTS

1. Dig up three small weeds, such as dandelions.
2. Plant each of them in separate plastic pots with some earth.
3. Water one plant with fresh water from the tap.
4. Water one plant with salt water.
5. Don't give the other plant any water at all.
6. Look at the plants the next day. What has happened to them?

Liquid water

Rivers and lakes are filled with water in its liquid form. Liquid water can be poured. A liquid takes up the shape of the container it has been poured into.

What happens to liquid water that is not in a container?

Water always flows downwards.

Look, I can see some of the stones.

 MAKE A MOUNTAIN STREAM

1. Outside, make a pile of earth in the shape of a mountain and bury some stones of different sizes in it.
2. Use a watering can to pour water over your mountain.

Can you see little streams and rivers forming? Does the water carry the stones down the mountain?

Yes, the water is carrying the earth away.

You'd never believe it but...

You can tell the time by watching water flow! The Chinese used to tell the time by measuring how long it took water to flow downwards from one bowl to another.

Water flowing over rough rocks wears them down into smooth pebbles. Small stones and pebbles can be carried along by water.

Over many thousands of years, a fast-flowing river can cut a deep valley through a landscape.

Solid water

The water that pours out of your tap is liquid, but when water freezes, it becomes ice which is solid. Ice floats because it is lighter than water. Icebergs as big as skyscrapers float in the sea. Did you know that most of the iceberg is hidden under the water?

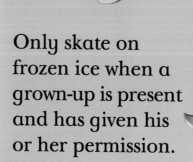

Why can't we skate here in the warm weather?

In the winter, when it is very cold, water in the clouds freezes into crystals of ice or snowflakes. Each snowflake is a different shape but they all have six sides.

Only skate on frozen ice when a grown-up is present and has given his or her permission.

When it gets warmer ice begins to melt. It turns back into water.

The ice will have melted.

GETTING BIGGER
When liquid water freezes into ice it gets bigger.
1. Pour equal amounts of water into two plastic bottles, to three-quarters full.
2. On the outside of the jars mark where the water level is.
3. Put one bottle in the freezer overnight. What has happened to the water level in the frozen bottle?

You'd never believe it but...
Most of the fresh water on Earth is frozen! It is frozen in huge ice caps around the North and South Poles. It is so cold here that the snow and ice never melt.

Water in the air

The air around you is full of tiny droplets of water, too small to see or feel. These droplets are a gas called water vapour.

    When water from seas, lakes, rivers and puddles dries out in the sunshine it becomes water vapour in the air. This process is called evaporation.

The water I left out yesterday has disappeared.

You'd never believe it but...

Boiling water and steam can burst straight out of the ground. These hot springs are called geysers.

Water heating up in a saucepan begins to bubble. When the water is as hot as it can be, it begins to bubble very fast. It turns into steam which is a kind of gas.

You can see steam rising from a boiling kettle or from hot water when you turn on the hot water tap.

Be careful. Steam is very hot – it can give you a nasty burn.

No it hasn't. It's in the air!

DRYING PUDDLES

1. After it has rained, go outside and mark around the edge of a puddle with some small pebbles.
2. Check the puddle an hour later. Is it smaller?
3. How long does it take for the whole puddle to disappear? The puddle water has become invisible water vapour in the air.

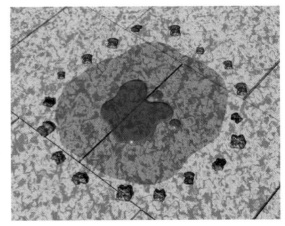

The weather

The Sun's heat makes water vapour from seas and oceans rise high up into the sky. The cold air there turns it into drops of water. This process is called condensation. These drops of water make a cloud.

The drops of water in a cloud join together and get bigger. When they become too big and heavy to stay in the air, they fall to the ground as rain.

Fluffy clouds mean we should have a warm sunny day.

When it becomes cold, water vapour turns back into liquid water.

Look out for drops of water glistening on a spider's web on a cold morning.

Sometimes you can see the water in the air all around you. On chilly mornings, the cold air turns water vapour into drops of water that look like a cloud on the ground. We call it mist, or if it is really thick, we call it fog.

Yes, but they might grow into storm clouds.

MAKING MIST

1. Put a glass in the fridge until it is quite cold.
2. Take it out. Carefully breathe into the glass.
3. Can you see any mist appear? The coldness of the glass has turned the warm water vapour from your breath into mist!

You'd never believe it but...

If you climb a very tall mountain you can walk in the clouds. Walking through clouds is rather like walking through mist.

The water cycle

Rain and snow fall on the mountains and collect into streams. The water in the streams runs downhill towards the sea, collecting more water from rain and other streams as it goes.

The Sun's heat dries up the water from the sea into the air, where it falls again as rain.

Do you think my stick will go all the way down to the sea?

When some of the water from the sea is turned into water vapour, most of the salt is left behind in the sea. When the water vapour falls again as rain, it is not salty, like seawater.

You'd never believe it but...

Dinosaurs drank the same water that you drink! Water is never used up. It keeps going round and round, being used again and again.

Yes, because the river will take it there.

FRESH OR SALTY?
1. Mix some salt and water together in a bowl.
2. Leave the bowl in the sunshine for a few hours. What has happened to the water? What is left behind in the bowl?

Floating and sinking

Have you noticed that some objects float in water and others sink to the bottom?

When you put an object in water it pushes down on the water. At the same time, the water is pushing back up.

My ball of modelling clay has sunk!

FEEL THE FORCE
1. Fill a bowl with water. Put a plastic ball on the water and watch it float.
2. Push down on the ball. Can you feel the force of the water pushing it up?
What happens when you let go of the ball suddenly?

Things will either float or sink, depending on their shape and how heavy they are.

You'd never believe it but...

Submarines can sink or float. They sink when tanks inside them are filled with water. They float when the tanks are filled with air.

I've made mine into a boat shape - and it's floating.

Mixing and dissolving

You probably use water to make mixtures every day. A glass of lemonade is a mixture of water and lemon juice. You can also add sugar if you like it sweet. Do you mix bath foam in your bath water to make bubbles?

Some things disappear when they are mixed with water. They are still there but you can't see them. This is called dissolving.

The sugar has dissolved in the water. I can't see it, but I can still taste it.

> I've mixed tea leaves with water. I can still see the tea leaves.

You'd never believe it but...

Stalactites like these take 500 years to grow just 1 inch (2.5cm). Dripping water dissolves the rock on the cave roof. Each drop leaves a tiny bit of rock behind and a stalactite gradually grows.

MAKING MIXTURES

Try mixing some milk, coffee granules, tea leaves, sugar, salt, honey and cooking oil in separate cups of water. Which ones disappear completely? Which ones change the colour of the water? Which ones don't mix with water at all?

Water in your body

Your body is mostly made up of water. Your body naturally loses water every day when you sweat or go to the toilet. That is why it is important to drink plenty of water to replace the water you lose.

Plants drink water too. They soak up water in the soil through their roots.

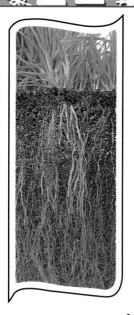

In the sunshine, or after lots of exercise, you may feel thirsty. You lose water through your skin when you sweat.

Do you want some water?

Yes please. I'm really thirsty!

Do you know where the water that pours out of your taps comes from?

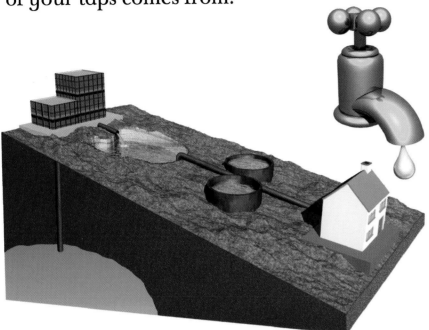

It comes from rivers, lakes or from wells deep under the ground. It can be pumped up and used for drinking and watering crops.

First it is stored in a reservoir and then it is cleaned at a water works to make sure it is safe for us to drink.

You'd never believe it but...

You can survive without food for quite a long time. You wouldn't be able to survive for long without water. There is very little water in a desert.

CLEANING WATER

1. Mix some water in a jug with some earth, small sticks and stones and bits of leaves.
2. Pour it through a sieve into a bowl.
3. What can you see in the sieve?
4. Pour it through some filter paper into a bowl.
5. How clean do you think the water is? The water we drink has to be cleaned many many times to make it safe to drink.

Washing

Have you ever tried to wash your hands properly using only water? It's very difficult because liquid water has a surface, like a thin, elastic skin.

Special chemicals in cleaning products, such as soap and shampoo, break the water's skin. This makes it easier for the water and soap to get rid of the dirt.

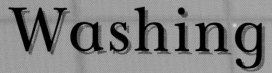

The water we use for washing gets dirty. Dirty water goes down pipes into sewers underground.

The pipes lead to sewage works where the water is cleaned before it is put back into rivers and the sea.

It's taking a long time to get my hands clean without soap.

You'd never believe it but...

Insects called pond skaters are so light that they can walk on the skin of water without breaking it. This skin is not very strong. Heavy objects pass straight through it.

My hands are already clean.

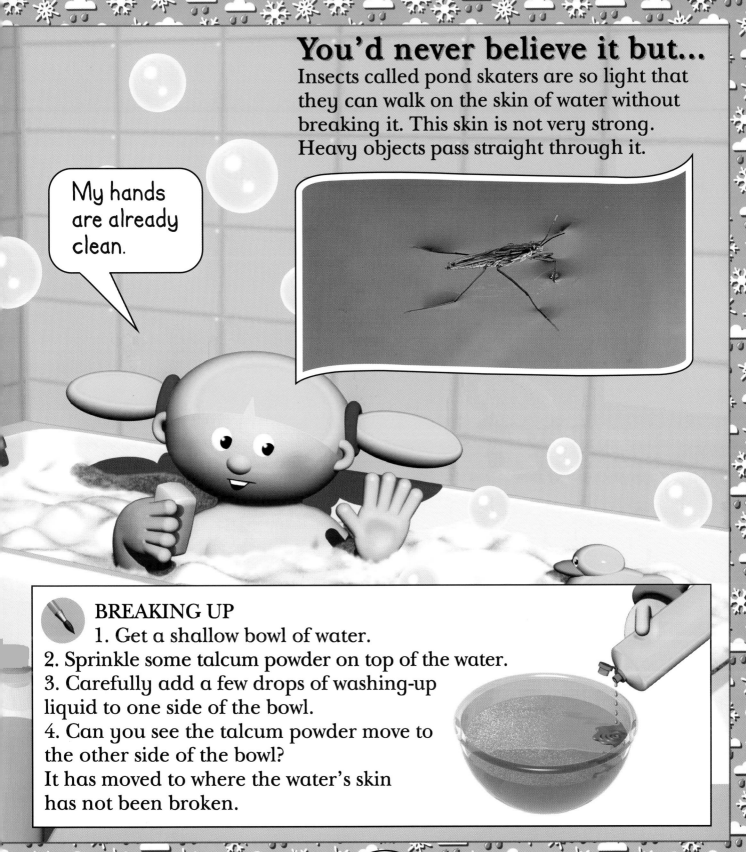

BREAKING UP

1. Get a shallow bowl of water.
2. Sprinkle some talcum powder on top of the water.
3. Carefully add a few drops of washing-up liquid to one side of the bowl.
4. Can you see the talcum powder move to the other side of the bowl?

It has moved to where the water's skin has not been broken.

Living in water

Have you tried swimming underwater? It probably wasn't long before you had to come up for air.

You breathe the air all around you. Fish, other water creatures and plants breathe air too, but they breathe air that is dissolved in the water.

Fish have a smooth shape that is good for moving quickly through the water. Is your body a good shape for swimming?

I wish I had a snorkel so I could breathe air.

Fish breathe air in the water through the gills on the sides of their heads.

These fish are just too fast to catch.

Dolphins and whales can stay underwater for a long time. When they come up to the surface, they breathe out through holes in the top of their heads called blowholes.

Plants which live in water are specially adapted so that they can survive in the water.

You'd never believe it but...

The blue whale is the biggest animal that has ever lived. It is even bigger than any of the dinosaurs.

Glossary

Dissolving

Some solid things like sugar and salt break into tiny particles and seem to disappear when they are mixed with water. We call this dissolving.

Electricity

Electricity is a kind of energy. It can be made in power stations and used to heat our homes.

Float

When different things are put onto water they may either float or sink. Things that float stay on the top, or surface, of the water and do not sink to the bottom.

Gas

The air all around us is a kind of gas that we cannot see. If you heat water in a kettle or a saucepan it turns into a kind of gas that we call steam.

Liquid

Water can be a solid like ice, or a gas like steam, or a liquid like the water that pours out of a tap. Liquids pour and flow and take the shape of the containers they are poured into.

Mixing

When you put two or more different things together you are mixing them. Water and lemon juice make a mixture you can drink called lemonade. You can add sugar to this if you like things to taste sweeter.

Planet

We live on a planet called Earth. Planet Earth is just one of nine planets which are enormous balls made up of rock, ice and gas that move round the Sun. These other planets include Mercury, Venus, Mars, Jupiter, Saturn, Uranus, Neptune and Pluto.

Seawater

All of the oceans and seas that cover most of the Earth are made up of seawater. Seawater is salty because it contains minerals and salts that have been washed off the land and carried to the sea by rivers.

Solid

Things that are solid, like a stone or log, have a shape of their own. Water is solid when it is frozen and becomes ice.

Steam

When water is heated and becomes as hot as it can be, it boils. It bubbles very fast and turns into a kind of gas. This gas escapes into the air. We call this gas steam.

Vapour

When water from the sea, lakes and puddles dries out in the warm sun, it becomes tiny droplets of water in the air too small to see. This is called water vapour.

Water

Water is in the oceans, lakes and rivers and it pours out of your tap for you to drink and use for washing. It can be liquid that pours, solid like ice in the fridge, or gas like steam from a hot cup of coffee.

Index

A

air 5, 6, 14, 15, 17, 18, 21, 28, 30, 31

B

boiling 31
breathing 28, 29

C

clouds 12, 16, 17
condensation 16

D

deserts 25
dinosaurs 19, 29
dissolving 22, 23, 30

E

Earth 5, 8, 31
evaporation 14

F

floating 20, 21, 30
fog 17
freezing 12, 13

G

gases 6, 7, 15, 30, 31
geysers 14

I

ice 6, 7, 9, 12, 13, 30, 31

L

lakes 10, 25
liquids 6, 7, 9, 10, 30

M

melting 13
mist 5, 17
mixing 22, 23, 30

P

particles 30
plants 8, 9, 24, 28, 29
puddles 15

R

rain 15, 16, 18
rivers 6, 10, 11, 19, 25, 26, 31

S

seas 6, 8, 9, 16, 18, 26
snow 12, 18
solids 6, 7, 12, 13, 31
steam 6, 7, 15, 30, 31

W

water vapour 14, 15, 17, 18, 31
weather 12, 16, 17

PHOTO CREDITS

Abbreviations: t-top, b-bottom, r-right, l-left, c-centre.

Pages 7, 9r, 12, 13, 14, 17b, 26 & 28 – Frank Spooner Pictures. 8, 9l, 11 both, 16, 17t & 29 – Roger Vlitos. 21 – Solution Pictures. 15 & 23 – Spectrum Colour Library. 24 & 27 – Bruce Coleman Collection. 25 – Rex Features.